I Breathe a New Song

Poems of the Eskimo

I Breathe a New Song

Poems of the Eskimo

Edited by Richard Lewis   Illustrated by Oonark

with an Introduction by Edmund Carpenter

Simon and Schuster · New York

The poems on pages 27, 28, 30, 32 bot., 34-35, 36, 37, 40 top, 43, 54-55, 62 top, 67, 68, 69, 71
top, 93, 96-97, 100 bot., 106, 110-111 top, 112, 115 bot., and 122-123 are used by permission of
Rudolf Sand, Denmark, counsel for the estate of Knud Rasmussen.

The poems on pages 88 and 111 bot., from *The Unwritten Song*, vol. 1, by Willard R. Trask,
copyright © 1966 by Willard R. Trask, are reprinted by permission of The Macmillan Company
and Jonathan Cape, Ltd.

The poems on pages 118 bot. and 120 bot., from *Anerca*, edited by Edmund Carpenter, copyright © 1959 by Edmund Carpenter, are reprinted by permission of J. M. Dent & Sons, Toronto,
Canada.

The poem on page 120 top, from *Selected Translations*, by W. S. Merwin, copyright © 1968
by W. S. Merwin, is reprinted by permission of Atheneum Publishers.

The poem on page 119, from *Book of the Eskimos*, by Peter Freuchen, edited by Dagmar
Freuchen, copyright © 1961 by Peter Freuchen Estate, is reprinted by permission of The World
Publishing Company and Harold Matson Company, Inc.

The poem on page 114, from *Primitive Songs*, by Clarence Maurice Bowra, copyright © 1962
by C. M. Bowra, is reprinted by permission of The World Publishing Company and George Weiden-
feld & Nicolson Ltd.

The poems on pages 60 center, 62 bot., 63, 84 bot., and 115 top, from *Poèmes Eskimos*, by
Paul-Emile Victor, were translated by Charlene Slivnick and are used by permission of Editions
Seghers. Translations copyright © 1971 by Charlene Slivnick.

The poems on pages 31, 44 top, 49, 50, 56, 72 bot., 75, 77, 78, 94-95, 99, and 100 top, from
"Songs of the Copper Eskimo," *Report of the Canadian Arctic Expedition 1913-1918*, vol. 14, by
Helen Roberts and Diamond Jenness, F. A. Ackland, Ottawa, Canada, 1925, are reproduced by per-
mission of Information Canada.

The poems on pages 79, 83, 104-105, and 107, from *Poèmes Eskimos*, by Paul-Emile Victor,
were translated by W. S. Merwin and are used by permission of Editions Seghers. Translations
copyright © 1971 by W. S. Merwin.

The poems on pages 29, 76, and 98, from *Canadian Eskimo Art, Northern Welfare '62*, are
reproduced by permission of Information Canada.

The poems on pages 44 bot. and 51, from the Laura Boulton Collection of Traditional and
Liturgical Music, Columbia University, New York, are used by permission of Dr. Laura Boulton.

With the hope that these songs
tell us always of our own spirit
that must sing

R. L.

EDITOR'S NOTE

This book grew out of my interest in the literature of indigenous peoples and the subsequent research I did for my collection of primitive song and poetry entitled *Out of the Earth I Sing*. While gathering material for that book, I became intrigued by the quality of much of the Eskimo poetry I came across. But to my surprise, there was no one collection exclusively devoted to presenting a cross section of Eskimo poetry. Because of this, and because of the profound role that song and poetic activity has played in the lives of these people, I decided to gather a representative collection of their work.

My hope is that this collection will help preserve a culture that began to disappear in 1955, when encounter with modern technology, information, and life patterns began to destroy Eskimo life as it had been lived for over 1,300 years, and as it is described in this book.

In undertaking this project I have been most fortunate in having the assistance of many organizations and persons who have been extremely helpful and generous with their time. I would like to take this opportunity to thank in particular the staff of the Frederick Lewis Allen Memorial room of the New York Public Library, who helped me track down a large number of sources; Dr. Laura Boulton, who allowed me to make use of her extensive collection of tapes and music of indigenous peoples at Columbia University; Mrs. Alma Houston of the Canadian Arctic Producers, Ltd., who first showed me and later obtained the drawings of Oonark for use in this book; Mr. W. T. Larmour of the Department of Indian Affairs and Northern Development in Ottawa, Canada, for his advice; Mr. James McNeill, of the same organization, for his help in obtaining poetry by contemporary Eskimo poets; Mr. W. S. Merwin and Miss

Charlene Slivnick, for their translations of poems from *Poèmes Eskimos* by Paul-Emile Victor; Miss Jane Lippe for her typing; Miss Anne Stephenson for her fine editorial work; and Mr. Edmund Carpenter for his illuminating and thoughtful introduction.

Most of the poems, except for a few contemporary selections, are anonymous, but the Eskimo group or geographical origin of each is known and appears with the poem: The Nunivak who take their name from an island just off the western coast of Alaska, the Copper Eskimos who inhabit Victoria Island, the Netsilik of the Canadian mainland south of Somerset Island in the Arctic Ocean, the Aivilik of Southampton Island, the Caribou Eskimos who live near the northwestern shores of Hudson Bay, and the Iglulik who live on Baffin Island and Melville Peninsula. The Thule and the Ammassalik are Greenland Eskimos and the Siberian live above the Arctic Circle on the Russian side of the Bering Strait. In addition to the poetry that has come from these diverse groups, I have included a few pieces which were translated from the original Eskimo into prose.

RICHARD LEWIS

7

CONTENTS

The Arctic is a hard land. It is snow-covered most of the year. The earth never thaws. Winds exceed seventy miles an hour.

Yet, when life there is reduced to its barest essentials, poetry turns out to be among those essentials.

The Eskimo word for "to make poetry" is the word for "to breathe." It is a form of the word *anerca,* the soul, that which is eternal, the breath of life. A poem is words infused with breath or spirit: "Let me breathe of it," says the poet-maker and then begins: "One has put his poem in order on the threshold of his tongue."

"My Breath—this is what I call this song," said Orpingalik, "for it is just as necessary to me to sing it as it is to breathe," and then began: "I will sing this song, / A song that is strong. . . ."

"Songs," he added, "are thoughts, sung out with the breath when people are moved by great forces and ordinary speech no longer suffices. Man is moved just like the ice floe sailing here and there out in the current. His thoughts are driven by a flowing force when he feels joy, when he feels sorrow. Thoughts can wash over him like a flood, making his blood come in gasps, and his heart throb. Something, like an abatement in the weather, will keep him thawed up. And then it will happen that we, who always think we are small, will feel still smaller. And we will fear to use words. But it will happen that the words we need will come of themselves. When the words we want to use shoot up of themselves—we get a new song."

Uvavnuk, delighting in the joy of simply being moved by nature, sang:

The great sea
Has sent me adrift.
It moves me
As the weed in a great river.
Earth and the great weather
Move me,
Have carried me away
And move my inward parts with joy.

Here the phrase translated as "moves me" also means "to be in a natural state"; to be moved by nature is to be in nature, to belong there. Emotions are expressed as physical responses: anger—*loosening bowels;* fear—*tightening sinews;* joy—*floating viscera.* Man is small, no more than a weed moved endlessly by the current, but intensely aware of forces acting upon him, and delighting in even the most trivial:

And I think over again
My small adventures
When with a shore wind I drifted out
In my kayak
And thought I was in danger.
My fears,
Those small ones
That I thought so big
For all the vital things
I had to get and to reach.

And yet, there is only
One great thing,

The only thing:
To live to see in huts and on journeys
The great day that dawns,
And the light that fills the world.

Toothless Kuilasar, an elderly Eskimo, told of starvation, of children born and husbands lost, of new lands and faces, and concluded, "How happy I have been! How good life has been to me!" She hadn't conquered life nor been rewarded by it, but life had acted upon her, spoken through her, and this was joy.

Eskimos wed themselves to nature. Nature's forms, they believe, all lie hidden until man reveals them one by one.

This is difficult for us to conceive, for our language emphasizes nouns, things already there, set apart from us, all clearly defined and easily seen. The Eskimo language, by contrast, makes little distinction between nouns and verbs; rather, all words are forms of the verb "to be," which itself is lacking in Eskimo. That is, all words proclaim in themselves their own existence.

The Eskimo language doesn't simply name things which already exist. Rather, it brings things-actions (nouns-verbs) into being as it goes along. This idea is reflected in the practice of naming a child at birth: When the mother is in labor, an old woman stands around and says as many different eligible names as she can think of. The child comes out of the womb when its name is called. Thus the naming and the giving birth to the new thing are inextricably bound together.

There really is no such thing as Eskimo poetry; there are only poetic acts by individual Eskimos. The poetry-making matters, not the result. And, since the *forms* of poetry are traditional, known to everyone, what need is there to keep examples? Like carvings, poems are created, not preserved.

As the carver holds the unworked ivory lightly in his hand, turning it this way and that, he whispers, "Who are you? Who hides there?" And then: "Ah, Seal!" He rarely sets out to carve, say, a seal, but picks up the ivory, examines it to find its hidden form and, if that's not immediately apparent, carves aimlessly until he sees it, humming or chanting as he works. Then he brings it out: Seal, hidden, emerges. It was always there. He didn't create it: he released it; he helped it step forth.

Eskimos have no real equivalents to our words "create" or "make." Their closest term means "to work on." The carver never attempts to force the ivory into uncharacteristic forms but responds to the material as it tries to be itself, and thus the carving is continually modified as the ivory has its say.

This is the Eskimo attitude toward not only ivory, but toward all things, especially people: parent toward child, husband toward wife.

It is also their attitude toward nature. Language is the principal tool with which the Eskimos make the natural world a human world. They use many words for "snow" which permit fine distinctions, not simply because they are much concerned with snow, but because snow takes its form from the actions in which it participates: sledding, falling, igloo-building. Different kinds of snow are brought into existence by the Eskimos as they experience their environment and speak; words do not label things already there. Words are like the knife of the carver: they free the idea, the thing, from the general formlessness of the outside. As a man speaks, not only is his language in a state of birth, but also the very thing about which he is talking.

Poet, like carver, releases form from the bonds of formlessness: he brings it forth into consciousness. He must reveal form in order to protest against a universe that is formless, and the form he reveals should be beautiful.

The environment encourages the Eskimos to think in this fashion. To Western minds the "monotony" of snow, ice and sky can often be depressing, even frightening. Nothing in particular stands out; there is no scenery in the sense in which we use the term.

But the Eskimos do not see it this way. They are not interested in scenery, but in action. This is true to some extent of many people, but it is almost of necessity true for the Eskimos, for nothing in their world easily defines itself or is separable from the general background. What exists, the Eskimos themselves must struggle to bring into existence. Theirs is a world which has to be conquered with each statement and act, each song and carving—but which, with each act accomplished, is as quickly lost. Carvings are discarded after being made, and

> Words fade away,
> Like hills in fog.

The secret of conquering a world greater than himself is not known to the Eskimo. But his role is not passive. He reveals form; he cancels nothingness.

Eskimos seem to be saying that nature is there, but man alone can free it from its dormant state; that it requires a creative human act before the world explored becomes a world revealed; that the universe acquires form, "existence," only through man the revealer: he who releases life inherent in nature and guides its expression into beautiful forms.

Here, then, is a world of chaos and chance, a meaningless whirl of cold and white; man alone can give it meaning—its form does not come ready-made. It is, above all, the poet who brings order and beauty to a world otherwise unlivable.

his own version, all equally true, for this myth is too complex for any single telling.

Sedna or Nuliajuk (young girl) rejected all suitors until a stranger induced her to elope with him. He was, in fact, a cruel bird disguised as a man, but she discovered this only after reaching her new home on a distant island.

Escape was impossible until one day when her family came to visit her. Her husband always refused to let her leave the tent, except to go to the toilet, and even then he tied a long cord to her. But this time when she went outside and he called to her, asking why she delayed so long, she had the ball of cord reply that she would soon return.

In the meantime she ran to the beach and joined her parents in their great sealskin boat. But no sooner had they set out to sea than her husband discovered the ruse and, revealing himself as a bird, swooped low over the fleeing family, turning the sea to storm, and threatening them with drowning. To save themselves, the parents cast Sedna overboard.

At first she clung to the gunwale. But her father cut off the first joints of her fingers; when she persisted, he cut the second and third joints. These sank into the sea to become the seal, walrus and whale that Eskimos hunt today.

In desperation, Sedna hooked her elbows over the side, but her father struck her with his paddle, gouging out an eye, and she sank into the sea, fingerless and one-eyed.

From the bottom of the sea, she now rules all creatures. Their floating bodies nearly fill her house. Periodically she sends animals forth to be taken by hunters, but only by hunters who perform rites and show respect for slain animals.

Other hunters return empty-handed. That is, Sedna withholds life from them, for they cannot survive without the food, clothing and fuel that come only from her subjects.

She is the most feared of all spirits, the one who, more than any other, controls the destinies of men.

In the various versions of this myth, Sedna is sometimes an unwanted daughter cast into the sea by her father, or a girl who has rejected all eligible men, or an orphan nobody wants; in one version she is already a mother, abandoned by her own children. In each, she is someone the family abandons for its own safety.

Abandonment of people is not purely mythical. Eskimo do, in fact, abandon old people. Killing newborn girls is common. And the position of orphans is precarious: one's own family always takes precedence. These are normal experiences in Eskimo life—cruel necessities forced on them by the scarcity of provisions.

The Sedna myth represents this dilemma, as Eskimos see it. They never asked that the universe be this way. But—*ayornamut* (it cannot be otherwise)—they accept life on its own terms.

They do more than accept: they take upon *themselves* the responsibility for the fact that life is the way it is. They give Sedna the power of life and death over man. Those who were forced to abandon her now place themselves in her power, dependent upon her good will, her respect for all life.

The hunter Aua, asked by a visitor to explain why life was as it was, took his guest outside and, pointing to hunters returning empty-handed after long hours on the ice, himself asked, "Why?" He then took the visitor into a cold igloo where hungry children shivered and into another igloo where a woman, who had always worked hard and helped others, now lay miserably ill. Each time he asked, "Why?" but received no reply.

"You see," said Aua, "you are equally unable to give any reason when we ask why life is as it is. And so it must be. All our customs come from life and turn toward life; we explain nothing, we believe nothing, but in what I have just shown you lies our answer to all you ask."

Hey, Up There!

When an infant is in its mother's parka, "up there," an intimate, poetic language develops between them. Some of these poems are designed for special occasions, the naming rite perhaps, to instill in the child a certain vitality, but most are simply word melodies between mother and child.

Magical Chants

Incantations, too, employ this musical speech, but with less variety in rhythms and tones. These simple prayers, spoken out into the air from some spot in the snow where no foot has left its mark, are, for the Eskimos, sacred words which in some mysterious way bring aid.

Recited in private, restricted in use, they range from household remedies to poems that are the very blood of the Eskimos. They are neither shouted nor sung nor whispered. The voice maintains a controlled tempo and medium volume but affects a strangely impressive, mystic tone, as if meant to be heard by one who is quite near and need not be summoned.

These chants or prayers contain a small group of words and expressions striking for their rhythms and tones. Some are sacred, taken from ritual language. About them there is, as it were, a veil. No theory of poetry, no science of ethnology, can ever really tell us what an Eskimo feels when he lets himself sink into the resonances and associations of these words.

Drum Songs

At intervals during the winter the community gathers in the dance house, the drum appears, and all the people arrange themselves in a circle about the performer. Drumming and singing, he moves slowly round and round the circle, knees slightly bent, sometimes hopping lightly on both feet, more often moving them alternately, without any attempt to keep time with the drumbeats.

Members of the audience accompany him in singing, but he remains largely independent of them, although he often tries to rouse them by his drumming and singing and by occasional whoops of joy.

Sometimes he passes his drum to another, thus freeing his hands. After awhile he ceases to sing and simply gestures violently, hopping and whooping with delight.

Each stanza of a drum song has a refrain and a burden. The refrain opens and closes the song, often with an added derisive shout or moaning yell last of all. Generally it contains one word of sense, but beyond that only one or two meaningless words which are repeated in varying forms.

Thus, the term *aja* is repeated and varied rhythmically as required by the melody, and once in a while is replaced by *ara* or *aha,* which are also varied. Unhampered by grammar or logic, the refrain is easily brought under the yoke of rhythm.

With the burden, however, the poet must shape meaningful language. He does this by rhythms and, to a lesser extent, by assonances and rhymes. Eskimo words and grammar lend themselves to metric cadences: iambi, trochees, dactyls, spondees, and anapests vary in an inexhaustible stream.

Eskimos are masters at recitation. They vary tempo, maintain intervals, and melodiously raise and lower their voices two or more notes.

Above all, they use their bodies, at times acting out entire scenes. A hunter may portray himself, the ice, the bear—yes, even the wind!

The Ecstatic Trip to the Nether World

The angakok, or medicine man, crouches beside his patient, chanting, sucking out the sickness, conversing with spirits he calls up in poems. His task is to cure the sick and save the dying.

If he fails and the patient dies, its soul goes beneath the sea to the home of the goddess Sedna. The angakok follows, traveling on the sound of his drum. A snarling dog blocks his path, but he paralyzes it with a chant and enters Sedna's strange house, confronting her directly. He beats her with a club, accusing her of taking the life of an innocent person. But this only angers her. And when he tries to appease her by combing out her tangled hair, she still refuses. Then he steps back and, with his drum held high, sings his song of life. Sedna is so moved, so touched by the beauty of his singing, that she releases the soul of the dying person, and the angakok returns with it to the land of the living.

All this takes place in darkness. The audience hears everything, but sees nothing. Before the séance begins, the angakok is securely bound and gagged, with his drum placed beyond his reach. Then the lamp is extinguished. Almost immediately drumming is heard, then strange voices, coming first from the angakok's body, then from the distant deep into which his soul has disappeared, then from the igloo ceiling. One spirit after another is heard, singing of its travels, of its work in the angakok's service.

The angakok, of course, is a skilled ventriloquist. But he tells no one. Nor does he ever reveal how he escapes from his bonds and gag.

Fighting by Singing

In East Greenland, Eskimos control feuds and resolve disputes by song duels. Two men—sometimes even two women—having become enemies, give vent to their anger once a year. With one drum between them they enter a small circle that has been scratched in the tundra, and take turns drumming and singing. Surrounded by an audience whose verdict is laughter, each seeks to direct this laughter toward his opponent.

Opening songs are often composed long in advance, even rehearsed in private. The introduction may be borrowed from some old, well-known song. The melodies and refrains may be inherited—property left by a father to his son, for example. But the burden is original, full of personal accusations, sneering references, word tricks and subtle allusions.

The duelist begins with a great show of modesty, then gradually unmasks his fire. He says one thing, outwardly innocent, but means something quite different. The audience understands and, unless the victim parries each thrust, matching point for point, he is soon laughed from the circle. The highest form of dueling consists in bringing your opponent to a full stop.

In the legend of Aaraatuaq, two enemies, having reviled each other in song through many years, at last become so used to it, so fond of it, they decide to continue their drum fighting after death. Aaraatuaq is the first to die. Then, when he hears his opponent approach his grave singing, calling him out, he rises from the stones of his grave and sings his drum song standing on the stones, using his shoulder blade as a drum and his leg bone as a drumstick.

EDMUND CARPENTER

PART ONE

With the Dawning Light

MAGIC SONG FOR HIM WHO WISHES TO LIVE

Day arises
From its sleep,
Day wakes up
With the dawning light.
Also you must arise,
Also you must awake
Together with the day which comes.

THULE ESKIMO

MAGIC WORDS

Earth, earth,
Great earth,
Round about on earth
There are bones, bones, bones,
Which are bleached by the great Sila*
By the weather, the sun, the air,
So that all the flesh disappears,
He-he-he.

Spirit, spirit, spirit,
And the day, the day,
Go to my limbs
Without drying them up,
Without turning them to bones
Uvai, uvai, uvai.

IGLULIK ESKIMO

*Sila: the spirit who represents the powers of nature.

MORNING MOOD

I wake with morning yawning in my mouth,
With laughter, see a teakettle spout steaming.
I wake with hunger in my belly
And I lie still, so beautiful it is, it leaves me dazed,
The timelessness of the light.

Grandma cares for me, and our family needs nothing more.
They share each other for pleasure
As mother knows, who learns of happiness
From her own actions
They did not even try to be beautiful, only true,
But beauty is here, it is a custom.

This place of unbroken joy,
Giving out its light today—only today—not tomorrow.

M. PANEGOOSHO
Pond Inlet
Baffin Island

MAGIC PRAYER

I arise from rest with movements swift
As the beat of a raven's wings
I arise
To meet the day
Wa-wa.
My face is turned from the dark of night
To gaze at the dawn of day,
Now whitening in the sky.

IGLULIK ESKIMO

WEATHER INCANTATION

Clouds, clouds,
Clouds, clouds down below,
Clouds, clouds,
Clouds, clouds down below.

COPPER ESKIMO

WEATHER INCANTATION

Only come, only come
Only come, only come.
I stretch out my hands to them thus.
Only come, only come.

COPPER ESKIMO

Glorious it is to see
The caribou flocking down from the forests
And beginning
Their wanderings to the north.
Timidly they watch
For the pitfalls of man.
Glorious it is to see
The great herds from the forests
Spreading out over plains of white.
Glorious to see.

Glorious it is to see
Early summer's short-haired caribou
Beginning to wander.
Glorious to see them trot
To and fro
Across the promontories,
Seeking a crossing place.

Glorious it is
To see the great musk oxen
Gathering in herds.
The little dogs they watch for
When they gather in herds.
Glorious to see.

Glorious it is
To see young women
Gathering in little groups
And paying visits in the houses—
Then all at once the men
Do so want to be manly,
While the girls simply
Think of some little lie.

Glorious it is
To see long-haired winter caribou
Returning to the forests.
Fearfully they watch
For the little people,
While the herd follows the ebb-mark of the sea
With a storm of clattering hooves.
Glorious it is
When wandering time is come.

COPPER ESKIMO

I will walk with leg muscles
which are strong
as the sinews of the shins of the little caribou calf.

I will walk with leg muscles
which are strong
as the sinews of the shins of the little hare.

I will take care not to go toward the dark.
I will go toward the day.

IGLULIK ESKIMO

O warmth of summer sweeping over the land
Not a breath of wind,
Not a cloud,
And among the mountains
The grazing caribou,
The dear caribou
In the blue distance!
O how entrancing,
O how joyful!
I lay me on the ground, sobbing . . .

THULE ESKIMO

PART TWO

You Great Long-tails

THE LEMMING'S SONG

The sky's round belly
Is clear without clouds.
It is cold, and I am shivering,
A-aye.

CARIBOU ESKIMO

THE RAVEN'S SONG

The male raven sings:
  When we happened to go down toward the sea,
  our wives said that their eggs broke
  and the young ones were frozen to death.

UNKNOWN

40

THE WHEATEAR AND THE SNOWBIRD

Whom can I get to husband,
Him with the lofty forehead,
Him with the many hairs (the shaggy one),
Him without trousers?

Me,
Will you have me to husband?
I who myself have a lofty forehead,
I who myself have many hairs,
I who myself am without trousers?

You,
I do not want you to husband
Because you have so lofty a forehead,
Because you have so many hairs,
Because you are completely without trousers!

Just as she said that,
At the same moment as she related that—
Quack! Quack!

WEST GREENLAND

THEN SAID THE BLOWFLY

Then said the blowfly:
"Because you are bellyless—perhaps
You cannot reply at all!"
The little water beetle then said:
"Devoid of belly—maybe so!
Still, you may be sure that I will answer back!"
And with a grimace
It turned its back at once
Without making any attempt to answer back.
He was a bad one for arguing.

NETSILIK ESKIMO

THE PTARMIGAN SINGS TO THE LONG-TAILED DUCK

You great long-tails
That love to splash about
Ducking down
Into the wet water.
You birds
That hover in flight
And never fly fast
And straight ahead.

CARIBOU ESKIMO

THE LONGSPUR'S INCANTATION

My parents when they left me behind, I,
Although I tried,
I could not raise myself from the ground
By myself.

My parents when they left me behind, I,
Although I tried,
I could not raise myself from the ground
Toward the lands.

COPPER ESKIMO

Somebody saw a crow flying by and asked him where he was going.
The crow answered, "I am going up to wring my grandfather's neck."

POINT BARROW, ALASKA

44

A SALMON TROUT TO HER CHILDREN

There by the promontory the kayak is coming out,
yayee . . .
The kayak-man's oars are red with blood,
yayee . . .
The white bone edges are red with blood,
yayee . . .
Oh, they have killed your father,
yayee . . .

NORTH GREENLAND

PART THREE

Harpoon of My Making

He constantly bends it, he constantly sends it straight,
The big bow, he constantly sends it straight.

He constantly bends it,
He constantly bends it.

Just as he seeks well for words in a song,
The big bow, he constantly sends it straight.

He constantly bends it,
He constantly bends it.

He constantly bends it as he walks along,
In summer as he walks along.

He constantly bends it,
He constantly bends it.

It is clearly easy to shoot big birds,
As he carries his pack walking along.

He constantly bends it,
He constantly bends it.

COPPER ESKIMO

Over there I could think of nothing else,
Beneath me when it breathed loudly through the water.

When the broth-provider was going to rush up to me,
Beneath me, I could think of nothing else.

While I had to give all my attention to the harpoon of my making,
It pulled me strongly upwards and downwards.

Over there I could think of nothing else,
The grub animal—I could think of nothing else.

My fellows went to lay low the caribou.
The caribou—I could think of nothing else.

Over there I could think of nothing else,
When the antlered caribou began to come to me.

While I lay thus in my pit and listened intently,
The antlered caribou began to come to me.

COPPER ESKIMO

50

First they shot a female caribou,
Then two buck caribou came along.
Their horns were just beginning to appear,
All velvet as in the spring.

CARIBOU ESKIMO

On his very first hunt
He killed a fine seal
Even in the dark.

AIVILIK ESKIMO

THE REAL SLAYER OF THE SEAL

How is it with him, your Alapa?
I have heard him shout for help,
When he had bound your catch, the hooded seal,
Shouting aloud
That he had bound a hooded seal to a little iceberg,
That he had slain it.
Your catch down there,
It was I who plunged my lance into it.
It flopped terribly.

NORTH GREENLAND

WALRUS HUNTING

The walrus, I harpoon it,
Stroking its cheek.
You have become quiet and meek.
The walrus, I harpoon it,
Patting its tusks.
You have become quiet and meek.

AMMASSALIK ESKIMO

52

SIGNAL SONG ON CAPTURE OF POLAR BEAR

I sing for a moment and vaguely
What I, and just today,
Have got the wish to tell of in my poem,
Have got the wish to mention in my song:
That on the way northwards, up there northwards,
When we went to meet each other,
That on the way northwards, up there northwards,
When we pursued and chased each other from all sides,
In singing my petting songs to get him to sleep,
That on the way northwards, up there northwards
   I overtook him and fetched him.

AMMASSALIK ESKIMO

I REMEMBER THE WHITE BEAR

I remember the white bear,
With its back-body raised high;
It thought it was the only male here,
And came towards me at full speed.
   Unaya, unaya.

Again and again it threw me down,
But it did not lie over me,
But quickly went from me again.
It had not thought
Of meeting other males here,
And by the edge of an ice floe
It lay down calmly.
   Unaya, unaya.

I shall never forget the great blubber-beast;
On the firm ice I had already flayed it,
When the neighbors with whom I shared the
   land here
Had just woken.
It was as if I had just gone to its breathing hole
   out there.
   Unaya, unaya.

There as I came across it,
And as I stood over it, it heard me,
Without scratching at the ice,
At the under edge of the firm ice to which it
   had hooked itself,
Truly it was a cunning beast—
Just as I felt sorry that I had not caught it,
   Unaya, unaya,

I caught it fast with my harpoon head,
Before it had even drawn breath!

NETSILIK ESKIMO

I wanted to use my weapon.
There was a big blubbery seal on the ice, even here.
I struck smartly with my harpoon,
And then I just pulled it up, the seal wandering from one breathing hole to
    another.

I wanted to use my weapon.
There was a big antlered caribou on the land, even down there.
I shot my arrow swiftly,
Then I just knocked it down in this place, the caribou that wandered about
    the land.

I wanted to use my weapon.
There was a fish right in the lake, even here.
I struck it smartly with my fish spear,
Then I just pulled it up, the fish that wandered about down here.

I wanted to use my weapon.
There was a big bearded seal, just at the river mouth, even here.
I paddled my kayak hard,
Then I simply towed it to shore, just at the river mouth.

COPPER ESKIMO

PART FOUR

Do Not Weep, Little One

TO OUR BABIES

My own little newly hatched one
Nestle close to me on my back!

AMMASSALIK ESKIMO

You are like an old wooden bowl
An old wooden bowl
An old wooden bowl we would lick
An old wooden bowl we would eat from.

AMMASSALIK ESKIMO

That she was taken out of her mother, thanks be for that!
That she, the little one was taken out of her, we say, thanks be for that!

AMMASSALIK ESKIMO

60

SUNG BY A LITTLE GIRL TO SOOTHE A CRYING BABY

Do not weep, little one,
Your mother will fetch you,
Mother is coming for you
As soon as she has finished
Her new kamiks.

Do not weep, little one,
Your father will fetch you,
Father is coming as soon as he has made
His new harpoon head,
Do not weep, little one,
   Do not weep!

                IGLULIK ESKIMO

He is round
He is radiant
Like a piece of ice in the water.
He jumps
He plays
Like a piece of ice in the water.
Aya aya yek!!
Lift your eyes
Look at me,
Little piece of ice in the water!

                AMMASSALIK ESKIMO

LULLABY

It is my big baby
That I feel in my hood
Oh how heavy he is!
Ya ya! Ya ya!

When I turn
He smiles at me, my little one,
Well hidden in my hood,
Oh how heavy he is!
Ya ya! Ya ya!

How sweet he is when he smiles
With two teeth like a little walrus.
Ah, I like my little one to be heavy
And my hood to be full.

THULE ESKIMO

PART FIVE

I Failed, Indeed, in My Hunting

MAGIC WORDS TO BRING LUCK WHEN HUNTING CARIBOU

Great swan, great swan,
Great caribou bull, great caribou bull,
The land that lies before me here,
Let it alone yield abundant meat,
Be rich in vegetation,
Your moss-food.
You shall look forward to and come hither
And the solelike plants you eat, you shall look forward to.
Come here, come here!
Your bones you must move out and in,
To me you must give yourself.

NETSILIK ESKIMO

67

The gull, it is said,
The gull who cleaves the air with his wings,
Who is usually above you,
You gull, up there,
Steer down toward me,
Come to me.
Your wings
Are red,
Up there in the coolness.

NETSILIK ESKIMO

Orphan,
You, little orphan,
On the other side of the open sea,
On its beautiful other side,
Creep there carefully,
Come out of the water,
In the shape of a seal,
Puh!

NETSILIK ESKIMO

CARIBOU HUNTING

All unexpected I came and took by surprise
The heedless dweller of the plains,
All unexpected I came and took by surprise
The heedless dweller of the plains,
And I scattered the herd
In headlong flight.

IGLULIK ESKIMO

COMPLAINT OVER BAD HUNTING

How is it with you?
Are you, I wonder, a man? Are you, I wonder, a real male?
My throw (with the weapon) is not smooth and firm,
I cannot get hold of the seals.
How is it with you?
Are you, I wonder, a man? Are you a real male?
These whales and walruses I cannot get hold of.

AMMASSALIK ESKIMO

PADDLER'S SONG ON BAD HUNTING WEATHER

I got my poem in perfect order.
On the threshold of my tongue
Its arrangement was made.
But I failed, indeed, in my hunting.

AMMASSALIK ESKIMO

I want to laugh, I, because my sledge it is broken.
Because its ribs are broken I want to laugh.
Here at Talaviuyaq I encountered hummocky ice, I met with an upset,
I want to laugh. It is not a thing to rejoice over.

COPPER ESKIMO

I am ashamed,
I feel anxious and perplexed.
My grandmother, she there,
Sent me on an errand,
Sent me out to seek.
Hither I have an errand
After the dear game,
After the dear foxes,
But I am only made anxious and perplexed.
I am ashamed,
I am anxious and perplexed
And my great-grandmother
And my grandmother
Sent me out to seek,
Sent me out on an errand.
Hither I have an errand
After the dear game,
After the dear caribou,
But I am only made anxious and perplexed.
I am ashamed,
I am ashamed and perplexed.

NETSILIK ESKIMO

74

Those game animals, those long-haired caribou,
Though they roam everywhere,
I am quite unable to get any.
I carried this bow of mine in my hand always.
At last I pondered deeply:
It is all right, even if
I am quite unable to get them in the present winter.

Those game animals, those seals,
Though they keep visiting their holes,
I am quite unable to get any.

I carried this harpoon of mine in my hand always.
At last I pondered deeply:
It is all right, even if
I begin at last to be greatly afraid in this present summer.

Those game animals, those fish.
Though I go out in the middle of the lake,
I am quite unable to get any.
At last I pondered deeply:
It is all right, even if
I begin at last to be afraid of the hummocky ice within.

Those seals, those fearful brown bears,
Constantly walking about here, I begin to be terrified.
This arrow of mine is fearless, this arrow.
Am I to allow myself to be terrified at last?

COPPER ESKIMO

I return to my little song
And patiently I sing it
Above fishing holes in the ice
Else I too quickly tire
When fishing upstream
When the wind blows cold
Where I stand shivering
Not giving myself time to wait for them
I go home saying
It was the fish that failed—upstream.

SOUTH BAFFIN ISLAND

DANCE SONG

Eastward I was idle,
On my journey north I was idle.

Bull caribou, cow caribou,
Because I could secure none of them I was idle.

Eastward I was idle,
On my journey east I was idle.

Edible things, bearded seals,
Because I could secure none of them I was idle.

Eastward I was idle.
On my journey back inland I was idle.

Black musk-oxen, brown bears,
Because I could secure none of them I was idle.

COPPER ESKIMO

DANCE SONG

I am quite unable
To capture seals as they do, I am quite unable.
Animals with blubber since I do not know how to capture them,
To capture seals as they do I am quite unable.
I am quite unable
To shoot as they do, I am quite unable.
I am quite unable,
A fine kayak such as they have I am quite unable to obtain.
Animals that have fawns since I cannot obtain them,
A fine kayak such as they have I am quite unable to obtain.
I am quite unable
To capture fish as they do, I am quite unable.
Small fish since I cannot capture them,
To capture fish as they do I am quite unable.
I am quite unable
To dance as they do, I am quite unable.
Dance songs since I do not know them at all,
To dance as they do I am quite unable.
I am quite unable to be swift-footed as they are,
I am quite unable. . . .

COPPER ESKIMO

My song was ready
it was in my mouth
it was all ready
my song
but I gave up the hunt
because the sea got rough
the cold north wind blew
and I saw heavy fogs getting up
along the mountain I saw them running
I saw them getting up
the cold wet fogs out of the north sky

AMMASSALIK ESKIMO

PART SIX

I See Your Face

THE DREAM

Last night you were in a dream
I dreamed you were
walking on the shore
over the little stones
and I was walking with you
last night when I dreamed about you
I dreamed I followed you
I thought I was awake
I wanted you
as though you were a young seal
you were what I wanted
as a young seal
in the eyes of a hunter
before it dives because it's being followed
you were what I wanted
that's how
I wanted you
in my dream about you

AMMASSALIK ESKIMO

I am seized with violent desire,
Alone by myself I become lustful.

I am seized with violent desire,
Alone by myself I become lustful.

AMMASSALIK ESKIMO

Above the mist
Beneath the sun
At the crest of the mist
At the foot of the sun . . .
And there you lie, asleep in the sun.

AMMASSALIK ESKIMO

I see your face.
It is always near me, though I
Am days away from you.
In dear memory, I always see your face.

I see your face.
Alone, in the dark night
I turn down the light and
In the darkness, I see your face.

I see your face.
You did not want to cry, but I
Remember now, tears as we said goodbye.
That is how I see your face.

I will see your face.
Only wait. When spring birds fly
Home to nest and mate, so shall I,
And I will see your face.

LUKE ISSALUK
Rankin Inlet
Hudson Bay

SONG

I found here for myself a woman. She walks much in an overcoat of calico.
She is a ruddy one, she is a pretty one.

NORTHERN SIBERIA

86

The wicked little Kukook
  imakayah hayah,
  imakayah hah-hayah,
Used to say . . .
I am going to leave the country . . .
in a large ship . . .
for that sweet little woman. . . . I'll
try to get some beads . . . of those
that look like boiled ones. . . .
Then when I have gone abroad . . .
I shall return again. . . .
My nasty little relatives . . .
I'll call them all to me . . .
and give them a good thrashing . . .
with a big rope's end. . . .
Then I'll go to marry . . .
taking two at once. . . .
That darling little creature . . .
shall only wear clothes only of the spotted-seal skins . . .
and the other little pet . . .
shall have clothes of the young hooded seal.

SOUTH GREENLAND

KAYAK SONG IN DIALOGUE

First man (on the rocks):
    Listen, you out there, listen!
    Listen, kayak, kayak, listen!
    Where, where, where is your wife?

Second man (in his kayak):
    I abandoned her, I abandoned her!

First man:
    But where, where, where?

Second man:
    In the women's boat, in the women's boat!

First man:
    But why, why why?

Second man:
    She was almost dead from cold
    And she was pregnant.
    She had her sealskin coat
    And I gave her a piece of fat.

First man:
    May the current carry her away,
    May the current carry her away,
    Far away,
    Into the distance!

AMMASSALIK ESKIMO

Great grief came over me—
Great grief came over me,
While on the fell above us I was picking berries,
Great grief came over me
My sun quickly rose over it.
Great sorrow came over me
The sea out there off our settlement
Was beautifully quiet—
And the great, dear paddlers
Were leaving out there
Great grief came over me
While I was picking berries on the fell.

AMMASSALIK ESKIMO

PART SEVEN

Fear Was About Me

HUNGER

Fear was about me . . .
In my little house
Remaining was intolerable.

Hungry and starving
I staggered in over land
Forever stumbling forward.

At "the little musk-ox lake"
The trout made fun of me.
I got no bite.

Onward then I toiled
To "the young man's broad"—
I had caught salmon there once.

I did so wish to see
Swimming caribou or fish in a lake.
That joy was my one wish.

My thought ended in nothing.
It was like a line
That all runs out.

Would I ever, I wondered,
Have firm ground to stand on?
Magic words I mumbled all the way.

COPPER ESKIMO

RELIGIOUS HYMN TO BE SUNG WEARING A HEAD DECORATION OF THE SKIN OF THE GREAT NORTHERN DIVER

Here I stand,
Humble, with outstretched arms,
For the spirit of the air
Let glorious food sink down to me.

Here I stand
Surrounded with great joy.
For a caribou bull with high antlers
Recklessly exposed his flanks to me.
—Oh, how I had to crouch
In my hide.

But, scarcely had I
Hastily glimpsed his flanks
When my arrow pierced them
From shoulder to shoulder.

And then, when you, lovely caribou
Let the water go
Out over the ground
As you tumbled down,
Well, then I felt surrounded with great joy.

94

Here I stand,
Humble, with outstretched arms,
For the spirit of the air
Lets glorious food sink down to me.

Here I stand
Surrounded with great joy.
And this time it was an old dog seal
Starting to blow through his breathing hole.
I, little man,
Stood upright above it.
And with excitement became
Quite long of body,
Until I drove my harpoon in the beast
And tethered it to
My harpoon line!

COPPER ESKIMO

95

BRING OUT YOUR HAIR ORNAMENTS!

Bring out your hair ornaments!
We are but girls
Who will keep together.

Hard times, dearth times
Plague us every one,
Stomachs are shrunken,
Dishes are empty.

Joy bewitches
All about us,
Skin boats rise up
Out of their moorings,
Fastenings go with them,
Earth itself hovers
Loose in the air.

Mark you there yonder?
There come the men
Dragging beautiful seals
To our homes.

Now is abundance
With us once more,
Days of feasting
To hold us together.

Know you the smell
Of pots on the boil?
And lumps of blubber
Slapped down by the side bench?

Joyfully
Greet we those
Who brought us plenty!

IGLULIK ESKIMO

I walked on the ice of the sea
Wandering I heard
The song of the sea
And the great sighing
Of new-formed ice
Go then go
Strength of soul
Brings health
To the place of feasting.

SOUTH BAFFIN ISLAND

98

My thoughts went constantly,
To the great land my thoughts went constantly.

The game, bull caribou those,
Thinking of them I thought constantly.

My thoughts went constantly,
To the big ice my thoughts went constantly.

The game, bull caribou those,
Thinking of them my thoughts went constantly.

My thoughts went constantly,
To the dance house my thoughts went constantly.

The dance songs and the drum,
Thinking of them my thoughts went constantly.

COPPER ESKIMO

DANCE SONG

My song, that one, it begins to want to come out,
It begins to want to go out to my companions, there
     being a request for singing,
There being a request for dancing.
My song, that one, it only, it also comes back, that one,
     my companions.
Asking to be made happy.

POINT HOPE, ALASKA

IMPROVISED SONG OF JOY

Ajaja—aja—jaja,
The lands around my dwelling
Are more beautiful
From the day
When it is given me to see
Faces I have never seen before.
All is more beautiful,
All is more beautiful,
And life is thankfulness.
These guests of mine
Make my house grand,
Ajaja—aja—jaja.
IGLULIK ESKIMO

100

PART EIGHT

I Am Tired of Watching and Waking

SONG OF AN OLD MAN ABOUT HIS WIFE

We were together
we were husband and wife
we loved each other
we're together
we're husband and wife
we love each other
we used to think
we were both good-looking

but a few days ago
only a few days ago
in a black lake
she saw an ugly face
a hideous old woman's face
all wrinkles
all blotches

she said I saw
the spirit in the water
the water spirit
all wrinkles
all blotches

whoever saw
that face before
all wrinkles
all blotches
haven't I
seen that face myself
don't I see that face
myself
when I look at you

AMMASSALIK ESKIMO

105

SONG COMPOSED AT THE BEGINNING OF AN AUTUMN FESTIVAL IN HONOR OF THE RIBBON SEAL

The autumn comes blowing;
Oh, I tremble, I tremble at the harsh northern wind
That strikes me pitilessly in its might
While the waves threaten to upset my kayak.
The autumn comes blowing;
Ah, I tremble, I tremble lest the storm and the seas
Send me down to the clammy ooze in the depths of the waters.
Rarely I see the water calm,
The waves cast me about;
And I tremble, I tremble at the thought of the hour
When the gulls shall hack at my dead body.

NUNIVAK ESKIMO

SONG OF THE OLD WOMAN

A lot of heads around me
a lot of ears around me
a lot of eyes around me
will those ears hear me much longer
will those eyes see me much longer
when those ears don't hear me any more
when those eyes don't look at mine any more
I won't eat liver with blubber any more
then those eyes won't see me any more
and this hair will have disappeared from my head

AMMASSALIK ESKIMO

YOUNG LADY'S SONG OF RETORT

How she has now become!
Like myself she has become,
She cannot even sing any more,
She cannot make drum songs any more.
As she has lost the ability to sing,
As she has lost the ability to make poems,
I have ceased to make songs,
I have ceased to make poems.

AMMASSALIK ESKIMO

IN THE SPRING WHEN THE SUN NEVER SETS

In the spring when the sun never sets
And when calm glassy waters roamed the
morning seas,
Oh, those were the happy times.

When the birds and seals,
Lived only for playing,
Oh, those were the happy times.

When we would stay up all night,
Looking for birds' nests,
Oh, those were the happy times.

When the sun began to warm the
morning air
And my sister could no longer keep her
eyes open,
Oh, those were the happy times.

When I, too, fought the coming of sleep,
But my dreams would win in the end,
Oh, those were the happy times.

LUCY EVALOARDJUAK
Pond Inlet
Baffin Island

AKJARTOQ'S SONG OF THE OLDEN DAYS

I call forth the song . . .
I draw a deep breath . . .
My breast breathes heavily
As I call forth the song.

I hear of distant villages
And their miserable catch
And draw a deep breath . . .
As I call forth the song
—From above—
Aya-haye
Ayia.

I forget altogether
The heavy breathing of my breast
When I call to mind the olden days
When I had strength enough
To cut up mighty caribou bulls.
I call forth the song
Ayaya-aya
I call forth the song.
I call forth the song
Aya-aya.

Three great caribou bulls I could cut up
—And have the clean meat all laid out to dry—
While the sun was on his upward way
Across the sky.
A song I call forth
As I draw a deep breath
Aya aye.

CARIBOU ESKIMO

TAUNT SONG AGAINST A CLUMSY KAYAK PADDLER

Oh, how I envy him for his singing
Every time I hear it—
What a sad failure I am, compared with him,
In the art of composing songs,
In the art of handling a kayak!

NORTH GREENLAND

Listen to my words,
All you children!
The kayak is very small
And dangerous;
Waves and winds have great strength.
But when your thoughts have become used to them,
You can travel among them.

Then first, like those who can do everything,
You will be good hunters of seals,
Like men when your need afflicts you.
On the lookout in the kayak you will strike with the harpoon,
And even in winter, when the cold is strongest,
You will proudly succeed with it.

Listen to the old,
The experienced counselor;
The orders they give to you
You must obey.

Even in winter, when it also happens,
You will proudly succeed with it.

WEST GREENLAND

114

SADNESS

When the sky to the North darkens,
When the sky to the North becomes covered
As if by an overcoat,
As if by an overcoat,
When the light dwindles,
When the light disappears
As if under an overcoat,
As if under an overcoat,
I think of my little children
I think of my poor children
And all is dark . . .
As if inside an overcoat,
As if inside an overcoat.

                              AMMASSALIK ESKIMO

Come in kayaks
Help
My body stiffens.
All my limbs stiffen
My legs stiffen
My hands stiffen
I, I am becoming stone.

                              CARIBOU ESKIMO

PART NINE

The Dead Who Climb Up to the Sky

Poor it is: this land,
Poor it is: this ice,
Poor it is: this air,
Poor it is: this sea,
Poor it is.

AMMASSALIK ESKIMO

WEATHER CHANT

Cold, Cold,
Frost, Frost,
Fling me not aside!
You have bent me enough.
Away! Away!

AIVILIK ESKIMO

You earth,
Our great earth!
See, oh see:
All these heaps
Of bleached bones
And wind-dried skeletons!
They crumble in the air,
The mighty world,
The mighty world's
Air!
Bleached bones,
Wind-dried skeleton,
Crumble in the air!
Hey-hey-hey!

IGLULIK ESKIMO

The dead who climb up to the sky
climb up steps
to the sky
up worn steps
all the dead who climb up to the sky
on worn steps
worn from the other side
worn from the inside
climb up to the sky

AMMASSALIK ESKIMO

Who comes?
Is it the hound of death approaching?
Away!
Or I will harness you to my team.

AIVILIK ESKIMO

120

SONG OF A DEAD ONE

Joy fills me
When daylight breaks
And the sun
Glides silently forward.

But I lie choked with fear
Greedy maggot throngs
Eat into my collarbone cavity
And tear away my eyes.

Anxiously I lie and meditate.
How choked with fear I was
When they buried me
In a snow hut on a lake.

When they sealed the door
Incomprehensible
How my soul could escape.

Greater grew my fear
When the ice split
And the crack grew thunderously
Over the heavens.

Glorious was life
In winter
But did winter bring me joy?

Worries corroded
Worries for sole-skins and boot-skins.

Glorious was life
In summer
But did summer bring me joy?
Ever was I anxious
For sleeping furs.

Glorious was life
On the sea ice.
But did that bring me joy?
Ever was I anxious
For no salmon wished to bite.

Was it so beautiful
When I stood flushed, embarrassed,
In the swirl of the feasthouse,
And the choir ridiculed me,
Getting stuck with my song?

Tell me, now, was life so good on earth?
Here joy fills me
When daylight breaks
And the sun
Glides silently forward.

COPPER ESKIMO

THE HEAVENLY SONG

I wonder if you were able then to sing?
When I rose up there
To the great heavens up there,
I had become frightfully exhausted,
I had become frightfully breathless.
But when I caught sight of my relations,
Is it you, who once were?
Then I took to singing high-soundingly,
That time I had been quite exhausted,
I breathed my little song about it.

AMMASSALIK ESKIMO

BIBLIOGRAPHY

Boas, Franz, "Eskimo Tales and Songs," *Journal of American Folklore,* vol. 7, January–March 1894.

Bogoras, Waldemar, "The Eskimo of Siberia," *American Museum of Natural History Memoirs,* vol. 12, part 3. E. S. Brill, Leiden, Netherlands, 1913.

Boulton, Laura. Laura Boulton Collection of Traditional and Liturgical Music, Columbia University, New York.

Bowra, Clarence Maurice, *Primitive Songs.* World Publishing Company, New York, 1962.

Briket-Smith, Kaj, *The Eskimos.* E. P. Dutton Company, New York, 1926.

Carpenter, Edmund, *Anerca.* J. M. Dent & Sons, Toronto, Canada, 1959.

Day, Arthur Grove, *The Sky Clears.* The Macmillan Company, New York, 1951.

Freuchen, Peter, *Book of the Eskimos.* The World Publishing Company, New York, 1961.

Houston, James A., *Canadian Eskimo Art.* Department of Northern Affairs and National Resources, Ottawa, Canada, 1954.

Intercom, vol. 12, no. 2, April 1969. Information Services Division, Department of Indian Affairs and Northern Development, Ottawa, Canada.

Malaurie, Jean, *The Last Kings of Thule,* translated by Gwendolyn Freeman. George Allen & Unwin, Ltd., London, 1956.

Merwin, W. S., *Selected Translations.* Atheneum Publishers, New York, 1968.

Northern Welfare '62, Welfare Division, Northern Administration Branch, Department of Northern Affairs and Natural Resources, Ottawa, Canada.

Rasmussen, Knud, *Across Arctic America: Narrative of the Fifth Thule Expedition*. G. P. Putnam's Sons, New York 1927.

————, *Greenland by the Polar Sea: The Story of the Thule Expedition from Melville Bay to Cape Morris Jesup*. William Heinemann Company, London, 1921.

————, *Report of the Fifth Thule Expedition 1921–24*. Glydendalske Boghandel, Copenhagen, Denmark.

    "Intellectual Culture of the Copper Eskimos," vol. 9, 1932.

    "Intellectual Culture of the Iglulik Eskimos," vol. 7, no. 1, 1929.

    "The Netsilik Eskimos: Social and Spiritual Culture," vol. 8, nos. 1–2, 1931.

    "Observations on the Intellectual Culture of the Caribou Eskimos," vol. 7, no. 2, 1930.

Rink, Heinrich, *Tales and Traditions of the Eskimo*. W. Blackwood and Sons, Edinburgh, Scotland, 1875.

Roberts, Helen and Jenness, Diamond, "Songs of the Copper Eskimo," *Report of the Canadian Arctic Expedition 1913–1918*, vol. 14. F. A. Ackland, Ottawa, Canada, 1925.

Thalbitzer, William, "Eskimomusik und Dichtkunst in Grönland," *Anthropos*, vol. 6. Editions St. Paul, Fribourg, Switzerland, 1911.

————, *Legends et Chants Esquimaux du Groenland*. Libraire Ernest Leloux, Paris, 1929.

————, *Meddelelser On Grönland*. Copenhagen, Denmark.

"The Ammassalik Eskimo Contributions to the Ethnology of the East Greenland Natives," vol. 40, part 2, no. 3, 1923.

"A Phonetical Study of the Eskimo Language," vol. 31, 1904.

Trask, Willard R., *The Unwritten Song,* vol. 1. The Macmillan Company, New York, 1966.

Trebitsch, Rudolf, *Bei Den Eskimos in Westgrönland.* Berlin, Germany, 1909.

Victor, Paul-Emile, *Poèmes Eskimos.* Pierre Seghers, Paris, 1958.

897.008   Lewis, Richard,
LEW   ed   72-427

           I breathe a new
           song

DATE			